LIFE ON A PIG FARM

LIFE ON A
PIG
FARM

by Judy Wolfman
photographs by David Lorenz Winston

LIFE ON A
FARM

Carolrhoda Books, Inc. / Minneapolis

We dedicate this book to the entire Eberly family—Barry, Pam, Alisha, Jocelyn, and Shannon—with our thanks and appreciation for their time, patience, and cooperation.   —J.W. and D.L.W.

Text copyright © 2002 by Judy Wolfman
Photographs copyright © 2002 by David Lorenz Winston

Carolrhoda Books, Inc.
A division of Lerner Publishing Group
241 First Avenue North
Minneapolis, MN 55401 U.S.A.

Website address: www.lernerbooks.com

Library of Congress Cataloging-in-Publication Data

Wolfman, Judy.
    Life on a pig farm / by Judy Wolfman ; photographs by David Lorenz
Winston.—Rev. and updated 2nd ed.
        p.   cm. — (Life on a farm)
    Includes index.
    ISBN: 1–57505–236–9 (lib. bdg. : alk. paper)
    1. Swine—Juvenile literature. 2. Farm life—Juvenile literature.
3. 4-H Clubs—Juvenile literature. [1. Pigs. 2. Farm life.]
I. Title. II. Winston, David Lorenz, ill. III. Series.
SF395.5.W65   2002
636.4—dc21   2001001637

Manufactured in the United States of America
1 2 3 4 5 6 – JR – 07 06 05 04 03 02

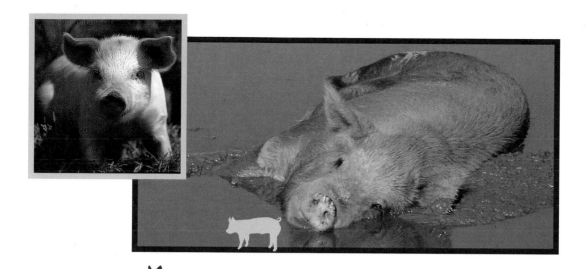

CONTENTS

MEET Our Pigs 6

Working for **PIGS** 24

Off to the **FAIR** 32

Fun Facts about Pigs 44

Learn More about Pigs 45

Glossary 46

Index 47

About the Author
and Photographer 48

MEET Our Pigs

My sister Jocelyn and I sit in the yard with two young pigs. I'm on the right.

Living on a pig farm is incredible! Where else could I watch the birth of baby pigs, see them take their first breaths, and care for them as they grow? It's a great feeling to know that I have a part in bringing these animals into the world.

I'm Alisha, and my life as a pig farmer began when I was nine years old. We live on my great-grandfather's 75-acre farm, and Mom and Dad wanted to think of a project we could share as a family. A friend of Dad's who raises pigs told us about **4-H.** He explained that 4-H is an organization that helps kids all over the world learn skills, explore careers, and help their communities. Members of 4-H do lots of fun projects— like raising pigs.

Even though my little sisters, Jocelyn and Shannon, were too young to join 4-H, I was excited. Mom and Dad talked with us about the work involved in raising healthy pigs and keeping careful records on them. They also made sure we understood that when pigs grow up, some of them are sold and used for food. We would have to be able to let them go when the time came. Raising pigs wouldn't be easy, but it would be a team effort. We said, "Let's do it!"

Once the decision was made, we all helped pick out six **piglets** (baby pigs) that were for sale at a nearby farm. We learned how to raise them as my first 4-H club project. The next year we went to a farm show and bought a pregnant **sow.** (A sow is a female pig that has already had babies.) We chose the sow carefully, because we had to pick one that wouldn't give birth until we were ready for a new family of pigs. Finally, we were official pig farmers!

Charts like this one help us keep track of when pigs will be born. Farmers must keep careful records so they know how many animals they'll need to care for.

BREEDING HERD MANAGEMENT PLAN

MAIN BREEDING HERD

When I met our first piglets, I knew I'd found the project for me.

A pregnant sow has to eat a lot to help her piglets grow.

9

When our sow had her piglets, we raised them and kept some of the females. Then we bought another sow, so we have quite a few of them. We also have one male pig, called a **boar.** When a sow is ready to mate and become pregnant, she goes into **heat,** and the boar seeks her out to **breed** her. About three months, three weeks, and three days later, the sow is ready to give birth.

Our boar is the biggest pig on the farm.

My sister Shannon checks the sow's teats for milk. The piglets are on their way.

We need to know ahead of time when the piglets are going to be born, so we'll be ready to care for them right away. We keep close watch over the sow, checking her often for signs of milk at her **teats**, which are also called nipples.

When we see milk, we know the sow is close to giving birth. If the milk is gray, the piglets will be born within twenty-four hours. If the milk is white, the sow will give birth within twelve hours, so we stay close to the barn to help.

A newborn piglet is covered with mucus, so it looks kind of gross.

We take turns waiting quietly for the first piglet to appear. When most animals are born, their legs are wobbly and they can't walk at first. But pigs have strong legs at birth. Sometimes the piglet practically walks out of its mother's body. Many of them can even run around the barn as soon as they're born!

After the first piglet has been born, we get to work. My job is to wipe the **mucus** from the piglet. Mucus is a slimy substance that coats the young pig when it is born. If the mucus gets into the piglet's mouth, the piglet could choke.

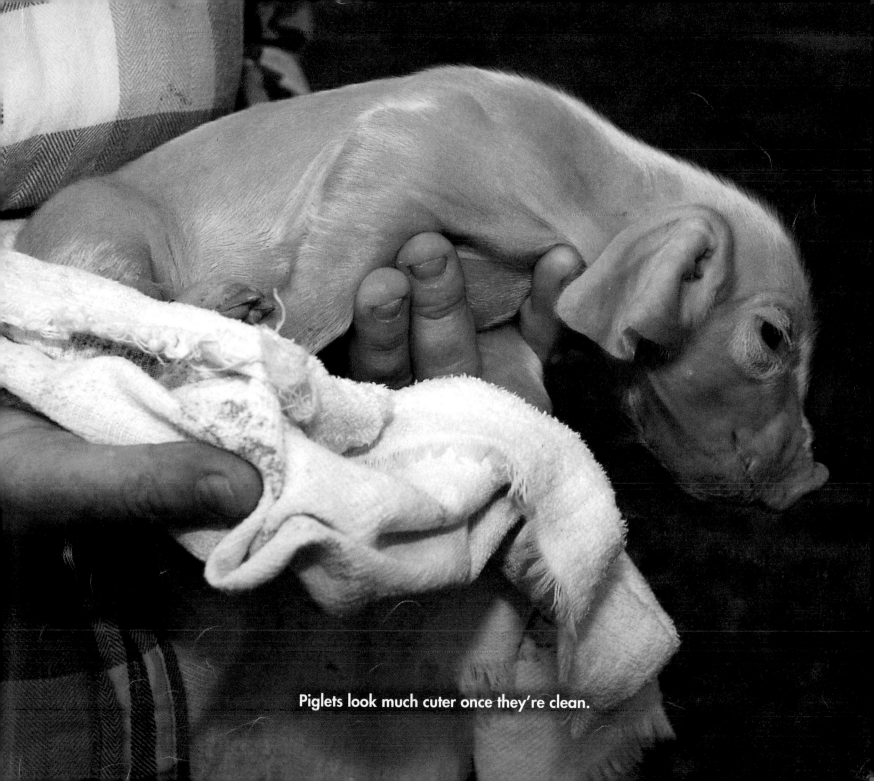

Piglets look much cuter once they're clean.

Once the piglet is clean and breathing well, we put it under a heat lamp to keep it warm. There the piglet snuggles in the hay and waits to be cared for. The next baby appears in about fifteen minutes. A sow can have as many as ten to fifteen piglets in one **litter.** Once one of our sows had eighteen!

Between the births, we do a few important things to each piglet. First we clip its two pointed upper teeth, called **needle teeth**, so they won't grow too long. Clipping the piglets' teeth protects the piglets when they bite each other while playing. It also protects the sow from being hurt when the piglets **nurse**, or drink milk from their mother's teats.

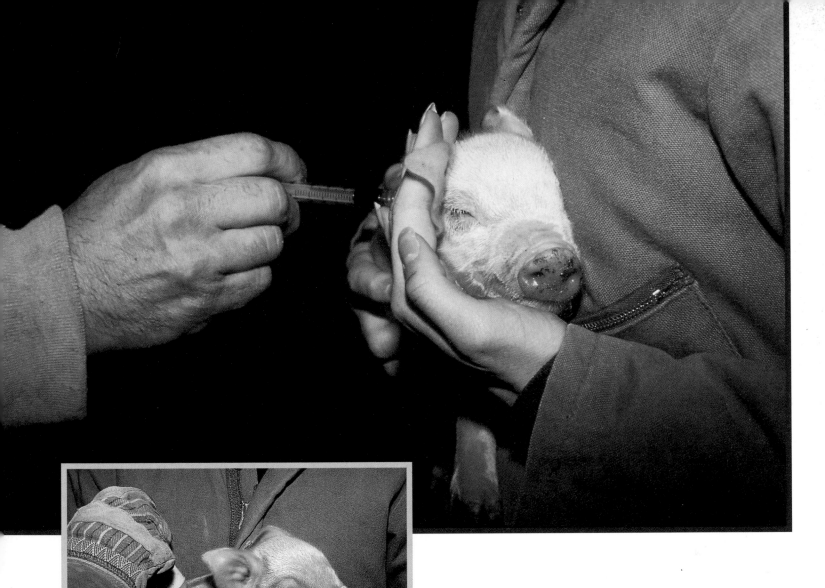

Next Dad gives the piglet a shot of a mineral called iron to get it off to a good start for a strong, healthy life. We mark each piglet so we know not to give it a second shot.

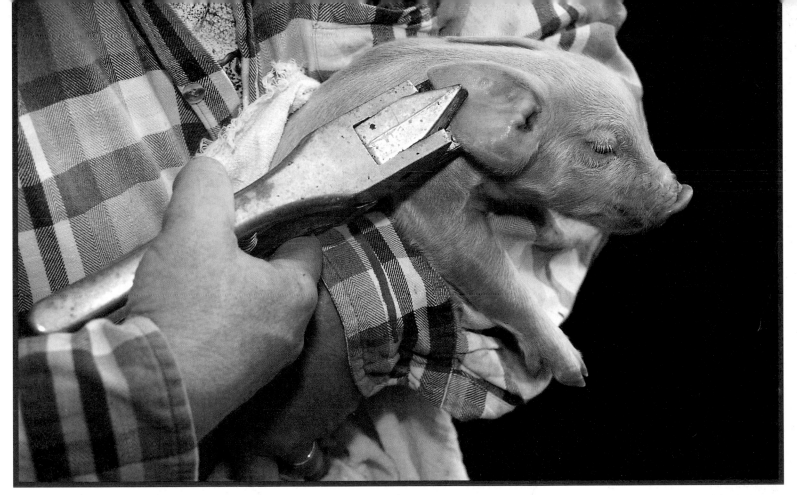

If we didn't notch our pigs' ears, we wouldn't be able to tell them apart.
It's good to know which piglet is which in case they get sick.

We also **notch** the piglet's ear for identification. We use a notcher, a special tool that cuts a tiny triangle into the ear. The first time I used the notcher, I was nervous because I thought the piglets might be hurt or frightened. But we're always very careful, and they don't seem to mind. Each piglet's ear is notched in a different spot, depending on the order of the piglet's birth in the litter. Notching helps us tell the pigs apart—some of them look an awful lot alike.

Shannon shows the newborn piglets how to find their mother's teats.

When three or four piglets have been born, we put them to the sow's teats. They nurse while the other piglets are being born. The sow gives milk for only about twenty seconds at a time, so a piglet nurses for a short while. It rests and returns to the same teat many times during the day.

A sow has enough teats to feed many piglets at
one time. That's a good thing, because many
litters have at least ten piglets.

19

Holding a newborn piglet is like cuddling a week-old kitten. A piglet is about 7 inches long at birth and weighs between 1 and 2 pounds. They're so cute! They're easy to hold, even though they are wiggly.

After five or six weeks, the piglets no longer nurse. They need more food, so we give them small pellets in a dish. These pellets are a mixture of vitamins, **proteins**, and minerals ground together. They work sort of like the vitamin tablets some people take. All we have to do is put the pellets in the dish, and the piglets come running to "pig out!"

Jocelyn helps two piglets eat their first meal of pellets.

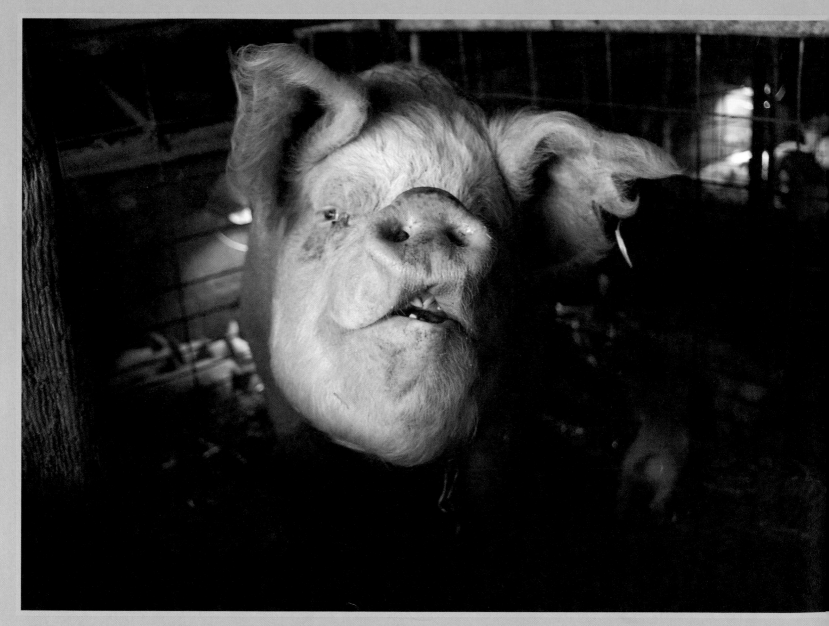

This mother sow looks happy that all her piglets have been born. Behind her,
you can see the litter of newborn piglets under the heat lamps.

Another newborn piglet searches for a meal.

A week after the piglets stop nursing, the sow goes into heat again. The boar finds and breeds her, and just about three months, three weeks, and three days later, she has more piglets. In one year, a sow might have two or three litters. She could become the mother of over forty-five piglets!

Working for PIGS

It's a good thing we love all our pigs, because we have to take care of them every day, all year long. It's hard work, but we enjoy doing it.

Twice a day, we feed the pigs a mixture of corn, barley, and ground protein. Dad feeds them on school-day mornings. My sisters and I feed them their evening meal, and we do all the work on weekends and vacations. We make sure the pigs have lots of water to drink. We keep the pen clean, too. It takes almost an hour to finish our chores, but the time goes fast when we all work together.

I feed the pigs every day. It can be hard to go out to the barn when it's cold outside, but our pigs depend on us.

We all help with the hay. Using a
pitchfork makes the job go faster.

Today it's Jocelyn's turn to
give the pigs fresh water.

When I go to the barn to feed the pigs, they often oink and run to greet me. Even if they're asleep, they seem to know that I'm there—they wake up and come to me. They're very friendly. I've even named some of them, so I can call them by name when I work around them.

Sometimes a pig looks like its name, like Red or Sandy or Buster. Other names, like Poochie, Patty, or Ten-Four, we pick just because we like how they sound. But since we have so many pigs, most of them don't get a name.

As we learned about pigs and their care, we were surprised by how smart they are. They eat, sleep, and toilet in three different areas inside and outside the barn. They like to have clean hay for their bed, which is why we have to clean the pen and give them fresh hay every day. When they need to go to the "bathroom," they go to one area of the pen so they won't mess up their living or sleeping area.

A happy, healthy pig would never go to the bathroom in the places where it sleeps and eats.

Most people think pigs are dirty animals because they like to roll in mud. But they don't do this to get dirty—they do it so they can keep cool. Human beings and many other animals can sweat to cool off, but pigs can't because they don't have **sweat glands.**

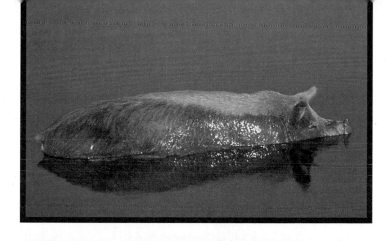

Since pigs don't have a natural way to keep cool, they roll in puddles. When the summer is hot and dry, with no rain, we have to squirt the pigs with a hose two or three times a day. If we don't, the pigs could get **heatstroke,** which could kill them.

Pigs grow quickly. Before long, they get too big to hold. But they're still fun to play with. When they're little, we give them rides in our wheelbarrow. When they get bigger, we have fun trying to stay on their backs while they give us rides.

This pig is so big and wiggly I can barely hold it. I think it would like to be on the ground, or at least in Jocelyn's wheelbarrow.

Jocelyn's pig would rather eat lunch than give her a ride. Shannon's pig makes a better "pony." It's almost as big as a pony, too.

When a pig is fully grown, it can weigh between 230 and 250 pounds. Boars can weigh between 400 and 600 pounds! That's as much as three or four grown-up people. While we raise the pigs, we are careful about their diet and try to make sure they don't eat too much.

Off to the FAIR

We raise our pigs to show, and sometimes sell, at a fair. This is where kids from all over the county or state bring their animals to be judged. It's an exciting time. Now I get to see how my pigs do against others. As a 4-H member, I can enter my pigs in several fairs each year, which is a lot of fun. Fairs give me a chance to travel and meet other kids my age who also raise pigs for 4-H.

Pigs will always follow a bucket if they think it's full of food.

About two months before each fair, we pick out the pigs we want to show. Show pigs are usually five or six months old and should weigh between 200 and 270 pounds. They shouldn't be too fat, so we put them on an exercise program. Every day I walk and run with the show pigs for twenty minutes. This gives me a good workout, too!

I watch the diet and weight of the show pigs carefully. If they're too fat, I give them less to eat. If they're too thin, I feed them more. I also spend lots of time poking the pigs with a whip or cane to teach them where to go when they get to the show ring. It's not easy to push around all that weight.

Dad and I work together to herd the pigs into the trailer. Jocelyn keeps an eye on them until we're ready to close the trailer door.

Finally, it's fair time! Dad backs the trailer up to the barn and sets up a ramp that leads into the trailer. The pigs usually go right up the ramp, but once in a while one will run off and have to be brought back.

When we get to the fair, we use hurdles to set up an aisle so the pigs will know where to go. We walk the pigs down the aisle to the stall that has been assigned to us. This is where the pigs will stay during the fair.

We usually go to fairs very early in the morning. Sometimes the sun isn't even up yet.

Pigs must be tagged so that they're shown with the right class.
Tagging helps the judges tell the pigs apart, too.

Pigs are shown in groups based on their weight. After we've settled in at the fair, the pigs must be weighed and tagged for the correct group, or class. Just before the show, my sisters help me get the pigs into the wash racks, where we scrub them with soap and water. We clean their ears and feet, and dry them with a towel. To make them look pretty, I shave their tails. Just before taking the pigs into the ring, I give them one last brushing.

Jocelyn helps me get our show pig clean and shiny.

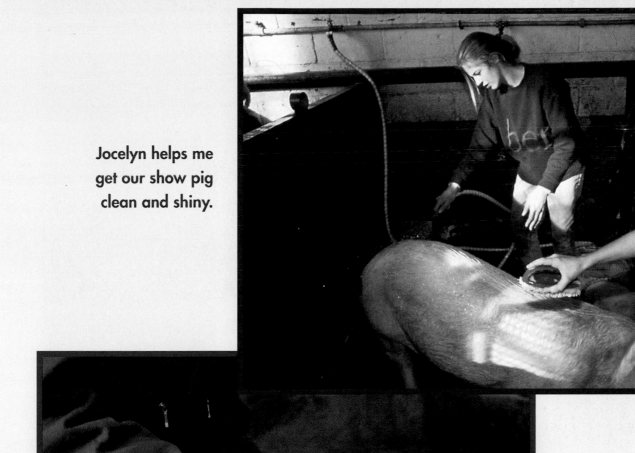

After the pig is dry, I use an electric razor to shave his tail.

37

The crowd watches as I guide my pig into the ring to be judged.

When it's our turn to enter the ring, I bring my pig in and walk it around so the judges can inspect it carefully. They're looking for a long, healthy pig with lean muscles, a large **ham** (thigh muscle), and well-shaped feet. The judges look at other pigs too, comparing them and trying to decide which will win.

This girl hopes the judge will like her pig best. Judges have had years of practice raising and selling pigs, so they know a lot about them.

At last the judges award a blue ribbon to the first-place winner, a red ribbon to the second-place pig, and a white one for third place. Yellow, green, pink, and brown ribbons are given for fourth through seventh places. My bedroom walls are covered with ribbons in all these colors!

Here I am at one of my first fairs, when I was nine. This pig won sixth place, so I got a pink ribbon for my collection.

Our family shows off Champ and his banner, ribbon, and plate.

Once, at the York County Fair in Pennsylvania, one of my pigs was named Grand Champion Market Hog! That meant he was the best of all the pigs at the fair. I was *very* proud. I showed the same pig in the Barrow Class, too. (A **barrow** is a male pig that can't breed.) He won again and was named the Best Supreme Barrow. After that, we named him "Champ."

When a pig is selected as champion, its owner receives a trophy, a plaque, and sometimes even a cash prize. The banner, plate, ribbons, and trophy I got for Champ are on shelves in my bedroom.

41

Though Champ is one of my favorites, I love all my pigs. There's something about the way they play, oink, and squeal that makes each one special. Just seeing them walk is enough to start me laughing, and I love their short, curly tails. Still, since I help raise so many pigs, I don't allow myself to get too attached to any one.

Jocelyn gives one of her favorite piglets a hug.

The saddest part about being a pig farmer is that after we show our pigs we have to send some of them to market, where they are used for food. I don't like to see my pigs go away, but I know that back at the farm, a new litter of piglets is waiting for me to help them grow.

Fun Facts about PIGS

Pigs eat **ONE-FIFTH OF THE CORN** grown in the United States.

Pigs use about 20 different oinks, grunts, and squeals to communicate with each other.

North America had no pigs at all until European explorers brought them across the Atlantic Ocean in the early 1500s.

WHAT'S THE PIG POPULATION OF THE ENTIRE EARTH?
Almost a billion in 1998—and more than half lived in China.

The largest known pig litter was born to a sow in England in 1993. She had 37 piglets!

Iowa has more pigs than any other state — **15 million,** compared with less than **3 million people!**

During the late 1980s, **Vietnamese pot-bellied pigs** became popular house pets in the United States. These intelligent animals can be housebroken, but some grow as heavy as 300 pounds!

The heaviest pig on record is a Tennessee boar called Big Bill. In 1933, Big Bill weighed in at 2,552 pounds and measured 9 feet long!

Learn More about PIGS

Books

Gibbons, Gail. *Pigs.* New York: Holiday House, 1999. This picture book introduces the physical traits, habits, and life cycle of pigs.

King-Smith, Dick. *All Pigs Are Beautiful.* Cambridge, MA: Candlewick Press, 1993. The author, a former pig farmer, reflects on the ways of pigs and offers a wide range of facts about them.

Miller, Sara Swan. *Pigs.* New York: Children's Press, 2000. Learn about different kinds of pigs and how they live around the world.

Pukite, John. *A Field Guide to Pigs.* Helena, MT: Falcon Publishing, Inc., 1999. Serious pig watchers can turn to this detailed guide to learn about the history of pigs and how to identify different breeds.

Websites

Breeds of Livestock—Swine
<http://www.ansi.okstate.edu/breeds/SWINE/>
The Department of Animal Science at the University of Oklahoma lists breeds of pigs from all over the globe. Color photographs accompany descriptions and historical accounts of the breeds.

National 4-H Council
<http://www.fourhcouncil.edu/>
Want to learn more about 4-H? Check out this fact-filled site for information about programs, news, and local activities.

National Pork Producers Council
<http://www.nppc.org/>
Stay in step with American pig farmers. Provides industry news and links to other pork-related sites.

Pork 4 Kids
<http://www.pork4kids.com/>
Run by the National Pork Board, this colorful site introduces viewers to different aspects of the pork industry. Play pig games, cook pork recipes, and meet kids who live on pig farms.

GLOSSARY

barrow: a male pig that cannot breed

boar: a male pig used for breeding

breed: to make pregnant

4-H: a worldwide organization that helps kids learn skills, explore careers, and help their communities

ham: a pig's thigh muscle

heat: the time when a female pig can become pregnant

heatstroke: a condition in which hot weather causes the body to collapse. Heatstroke can kill a pig.

litter: a group of young born at one time

mucus: a slimy substance that moistens a newborn pig's body

needle teeth: a pig's two pointed upper teeth

notch: to make a V-shaped cut in the ear of a newborn pig for identification

nurse: to suck milk from a mother's teats

piglets: young pigs

proteins: substances that pigs and other animals need to survive. Proteins help build muscles, carry oxygen around the body, and fight disease.

sow: a fully grown female pig that has already given birth

sweat glands: organs that allow human beings and other animals to stay cool by sweating, or emitting fluids. Pigs do not have sweat glands.

teat: a small, raised part on a female pig's belly through which a young pig drinks milk. Nipple is another word for teat.

INDEX

birth, 6, 8, 10–18, 23
boars, 10, 23, 31
breeding, 10, 23

care: of piglets, 12–18, 20; of pigs, 8, 24, 27, 29, 31, 32–33
cleanliness, 28–29
clipping teeth, 15
cooling off, 28–29

dangers to pigs, 12, 15, 29
diet, 20, 24, 31, 33. *See also* feeding; nursing
dirtiness, 28–29

ears, 17
exercise, 32–33

fairs, 32, 34, 36, 39–41
feeding, 20, 24, 26, 33. *See also* diet; nursing
food, pigs used as, 8, 43
4-H, 6, 8, 32, 45
friendliness, 26

grooming, 36
growth, 30–31. *See also* size

heat, 10, 23
heat lamp, 14
heatstroke, 29

intelligence, 27

judging, 32, 39–40

legs, 12, 39
litters, 14, 23, 43, 44

mucus, 12

names, 26
needle teeth, 15
nipples. *See* teats
notching ears, 17
nursing, 15, 18, 20, 23

piglets: birth of, 6, 8, 10–18, 23; care of, 12–18, 20; definition of, 8; size of, 20
play, 30
prizes, 40, 41

reasons for pig farming, 6, 43
record-keeping, 8

selling pigs, 8, 32, 43

shot, iron, 16
showing pigs, 32, 36, 39–41, 43
size: of piglets, 20; of pigs, 31, 32, 44
sows, 8, 10–12, 14, 15, 18, 23
sweat glands, 28

tagging, 36
tails, 37, 42
teats, 11, 18
teeth, 15

About the AUTHOR

Judy Wolfman is a writer and professional storyteller who presents workshops on creativity and storytelling. She also enjoys both acting and writing for the theater. Her published works include children's plays, numerous magazine articles, and Carolrhoda's Life on a Farm series. A retired schoolteacher, she has two sons, a daughter, and four granddaughters. She lives in York, Pennsylvania.

About the PHOTOGRAPHER

David Lorenz Winston is an award-winning photographer whose work has been published by *National Geographic World,* UNICEF, and the National Wildlife Federation. In addition to his work on the Life on a Farm series, Mr. Winston has been photographing pigs, cows, and other animals for many years. He lives in southeastern Pennsylvania. To learn more about Mr. Winston's work, visit his website at <http://www.davidlorenzwinston.com>.